THE FUTURE OF CODING

by Kathryn Hulick

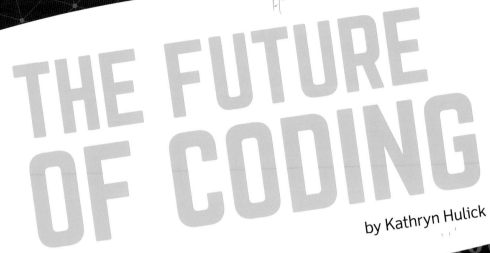

```
ay();
:query("SELECT DISTINCT(studio) as studio, COUNT(*) as count FROM image WHERE day.id = '$day->id' AND enabled='y' GROUP BY studio");
ysql::fetch($shots_result)) {
te::day_info($day->shot_date, $studio_list->studio,"quick");
= array("studio" => $studio_list->studio, "count" =>          ->count, "title" =>   ay_info->title);

mp_studio_list;
e] = $day;


t($date, $studio) {

al_studio_list)) die("error studio");
);
","shot_date = '$date'")       ie('date not found');


ECT image.id as image_i          age, image_date WHERE image_date.id=image.day_id AND image_date.shot_date='$date' AND image.enabled='y' AND i
($result)) {
tadate::get_copyright(          e_id);
te::get_models($image->im
d] = $image ;
```

FOCUS READERS

WWW.FOCUSREADERS.COM

Focus Readers is distributed by North Star Editions:
sales@northstareditions.com | 888-417-0195

Produced for Focus Readers by Red Line Editorial.

Content Consultant: Dr. Sherali Zeadally, Associate Professor, College of Communication and Information, University of Kentucky

Photographs ©: Africa Studio/Shutterstock Images, cover, 1; MMXeon/Shutterstock Images, 4–5; Zapp2Photo/Shutterstock Images, 7, 12–13, 16–17, 27, 29; one photo/Shutterstock Images, 8–9; Photodiem/Shutterstock Images, 11; KGC-268/Star Max/Ipx/AP Images, 15; Alexzel/Shutterstock Images, 19; Joana Lopes/Shutterstock Images, 21; metamorworks/Shutterstock Images, 22–23; Macrovector/Shutterstock Images, 25

Library of Congress Cataloging-in-Publication Data
Library of Congress Cataloging-in-Publication Data is available on the Library of Congress website.

ISBN
978-1-64185-327-9 (hardcover)
978-1-64185-385-9 (paperback)
978-1-64185-501-3 (ebook pdf)
978-1-64185-443-6 (hosted ebook)

Printed in the United States of America
Mankato, MN
October, 2018

ABOUT THE AUTHOR

Kathryn Hulick has been writing for children for 10 years. Her books include *Super-Awesome Science: The Science of Dinosaurs* and *Animal Engineers: Coral Reefs*. She also writes articles for *Muse* magazine and the Science News for Students website.

TABLE OF CONTENTS

CHAPTER 1

WELCOME TO THE FUTURE

A girl stands in the middle of a bustling city. She is on her way to visit her grandpa. She does not know how to get to his new apartment. But that's not a problem. The girl is in Singapore. This small country is a **city-state** island in Southeast Asia. Singapore is filled with many devices. Some help people travel.

The airport in Singapore uses touch screens to help travelers check in.

Others help people stay healthy. Each device has its own job. For example, a touch screen near the girl shows a map of the city. The screen helps her plan her travel. It even tells her when the right bus will come. The bus takes the girl to her grandpa's apartment.

The apartment is filled with **sensors**. Some sensors track her grandpa's movement. They send information to a **smart system**. If he falls, the system will call for help. Other sensors track how much water and electricity he uses. They measure how much trash he throws away. This information goes to a smart system that helps reduce waste.

Kitchen Power Usage

Power Realtime

419 W

0   3000

Light 1   Light2

15 W   12 W
0   5000   0   3000

Refrigerator   Range

289 W   103W
0   5000   0   3000

Kitchen Usage Today   1.2 kW

Smart systems can send information about power usage to a person's smartphone.

Code makes all these smart systems possible. Code is a set of instructions that tell a computer or device what to do. In a smart system, code helps each device send and receive information. People continue to create new ways to use code. They work to make life safer and more comfortable.

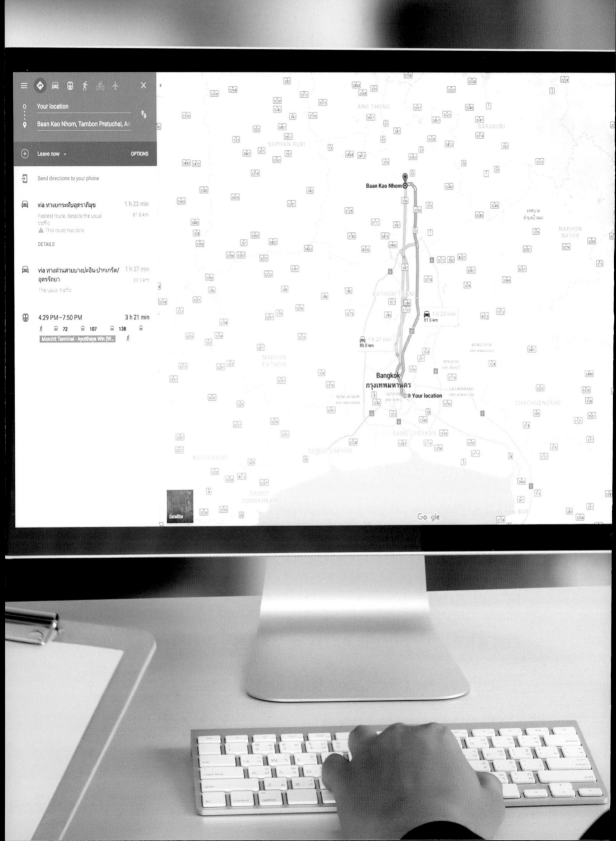

CHAPTER 2

THE MIND IN THE MACHINE

People use code to write programs. A program is a set of instructions given to a machine to tell it how to perform an action. People write programs to solve specific problems. For example, a mapping **app** gives people directions. The app finds the best route from one place to another.

Code provides the instructions that run apps such as Google Maps.

Computers and smartphones use code. So do robots. A robot is a machine that carries out a series of actions on its own. Every robot has a small computer inside it. This computer controls the robot's movements. People use code to write instructions for the computer. They

COMPUTER CONTROL

A robot's computer changes code into commands for the motors that move the robot. In many robots, sensors send information to the computer as well. The computer uses this information to help the robot avoid falling or crashing. In some robots, the computer can even make decisions. For instance, a self-driving car can follow a map without instructions from a driver.

People who write code are called programmers.

break each action down into step-by-step instructions. The computer follows each step of the instructions to complete the action. It tells the robot how to move or communicate. Changing the instructions makes the robot behave differently.

CHAPTER 3

CODE HELPS HUMANS

Robots can often be programmed to do jobs faster and more accurately than humans can. For example, many factories use robots. Each robot does one part of a process, such as building a car.

People can also write code that allows robots to do things humans cannot. These robots might explore dangerous areas.

Factory robots are programmed to do one action over and over again.

They might travel deep in the ocean or far into space.

In some cases, code allows robots to take over tasks that humans used to do. For instance, Astrobees are small, cube-shaped robots. They are designed to help astronauts on the International Space Station (ISS). Code allows

ROBOT ROVERS

Robots help scientists study other planets. Rovers roll across a planet's surface. They also take pictures of rocks. Scientists send code to these robots through space. The code tells the rovers where to go and what to do. Scientists have sent several rovers to Mars. In the future, robots may visit other planets.

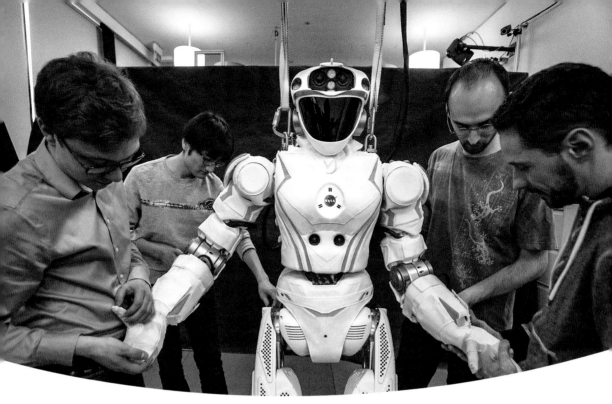

One day, code may allow robots such as Robonaut 5 to prepare a space station for humans on Mars.

Astrobees to do many tasks on their own. They can float around the ISS to check levels of supplies and measure air quality. They can find their way around without crashing. Someday, Astrobees might be programmed to take care of space stations while astronauts are away.

CHAPTER 4

A SMARTER WORLD

Many devices use code to gather **data** from the real world. Sometimes they share the data with other devices to form a smart system. For example, a self-driving car can sense other cars and people nearby. If a crash is ahead, the car could slow down. Then it could send the crash's location to other self-driving cars.

In the future, a smart system of self-driving cars could help prevent crashes.

These cars could find new routes to go around the crash. A system of cars might even help end traffic jams. It could keep cars moving at a steady speed.

Smart systems can help farmers, too. In some fields, sensors check the soil. **Drones** gather more data from above. They monitor crops to check for disease. The system uses this data to determine the best time to plant, water, or harvest.

Drones and sensors can also be part of the Internet of Things (IoT). The IoT is the network of all objects that share data. Each object uses the internet to send and receive information. The IoT includes thousands of devices around the world.

WAYS TO SHARE DATA

Farms: Sensors and drones monitor crops.

Homes: Appliances switch to a power-saving mode when not in use.

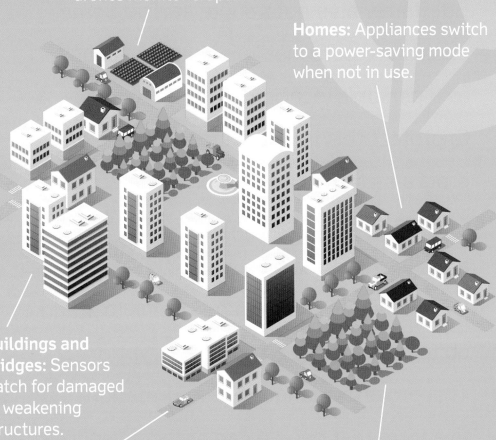

Buildings and bridges: Sensors watch for damaged or weakening structures.

Roads: Self-driving cars share information about road conditions.

Forests and rivers: Sensors monitor conditions and help predict floods or fires.

And it continues to grow. More appliances are designed to share information online.

The IoT makes people's lives easier. But it may also put people at risk. Some apps store personal information, such as a person's location. Programmers try to protect this information. They make programs that use passwords. However, criminals sometimes find a way to hack in and steal information.

Programmers design programs to stand up to hacks. They also use encryption. This process changes the information to a form that people can't read. Even if hackers steal the information, they won't know what it says.

Some programmers focus on cybersecurity, or strategies for keeping information on computers and websites safe.

As technology continues to spread, **cybercrime** will likely spread, too. Hackers may steal data. Or they may change the code to make a program harmful. Programmers continue to develop new ways to keep people's information safe.

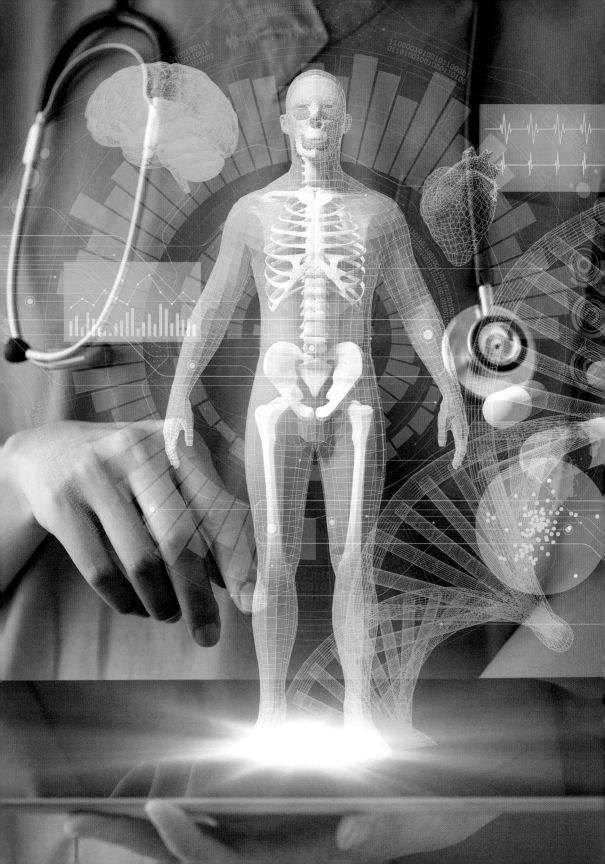

CHAPTER 5

WRITING ITSELF

As more devices join the IoT, more data will be collected. This data is valuable to coders. More data leads to better-informed systems that can make smarter decisions. Some smart systems rely on code that learns from data. The code can improve itself. This process is called artificial intelligence (AI).

Smart systems can help doctors diagnose patients.

Code that uses AI already impacts people's daily lives. Some devices use AI to recognize a user's face. AI can also translate languages. It can even help doctors identify and treat diseases. AI helps make programs faster and smarter.

A DIGITAL TWIN

Smart systems already share information to improve health care. In the future, they might help with treatment, too. Sensors on a person's body could collect data. They would measure things such as blood pressure or heart rate. A smart system would use the data to make a **digital twin** of the body. The system would show the body's organs and how they work together. Doctors could use this model to test treatments before trying them in real life.

As AI improves, people may not need to write as much code. Instead, a person would describe or perform an action. A computer or robot would copy this action.

WHAT AI CAN DO

Translate text

Interpret speech

Recognize faces

Identify images

Other machines could do more tasks with fewer instructions. One day, computers and robots may even be able to write their own code.

In fact, if AI continues to improve, machines might become more intelligent than humans. Scientists use the word *superintelligence* to describe this idea. Some people think computers and robots that are smarter than humans will be dangerous. They worry that these super-smart machines will be able to control people. But researchers are working to avoid this. Groups such as the Future of Life Institute help coders conduct safe AI research.

Eventually, robot assistants may help shoppers find directions.

As machines get smarter, they may replace some human workers. But AI has the potential to solve a wide variety of problems. It could even invent new technology. All these changes are made possible by code.

DEEP LEARNING

Many programmers use a technique called deep learning. In this method, programmers do not write out instructions for the computer. Instead, they create a network that works a bit like a human brain. This network can find patterns in data. Programmers can train the network to do tasks. Instead of writing step-by-step instructions, they have the network learn by studying many examples.

For instance, suppose programmers wanted to create a network that could identify animals in photos. They would start by showing the network millions of photos. Each photo would have a label telling the animal's name. The network would guess what kind of animal each photo showed. Every correct guess would form stronger connections in the brain-like network. These connections would help the network make

In deep learning, a computer learns to recognize patterns and categories.

more accurate guesses in the future. Eventually, the network would be able to identify animals in photos it had never seen before.

FOCUS ON
THE FUTURE OF CODING

Write your answers on a separate piece of paper.

1. Write a sentence summarizing the main ideas in Chapter 2.

2. Do you think creating smarter AI is a good idea? Why or why not?

3. What is the name for the network of all objects that share data?

    A. the program
    B. the Internet of Things
    C. the digital twin

4. Which is an example of cybercrime?

    A. making a website that requires a password
    B. teaching a computer to recognize different kinds of cars
    C. taking money from another person's online bank account

Answer key on page 32.

GLOSSARY

app

A computer program that completes a task.

city-state

A very small country made up of one city and the area around it.

cybercrime

Illegal activities done using computers or other technology.

data

Information collected to study or track something.

digital twin

A computer model that imitates a real-world object and can be used to predict how that object will respond to changes.

drones

Aircraft or ships that are controlled remotely or operate on their own.

sensors

Devices that collect and report information.

smart system

A group of devices that work together to detect and respond to changes.

TO LEARN MORE

BOOKS

Bedell, Jane M. *So, You Want to Be a Coder?* New York: Aladdin, 2016.

McManus, Sean. *How to Code in 10 Easy Lessons.* Lake Forest, CA: Walter Foster Jr., 2015.

Smibert, Angie. *All About Coding.* Lake Elmo, MN: Focus Readers, 2017.

NOTE TO EDUCATORS

Visit **www.focusreaders.com** to find lesson plans, activities, links, and other resources related to this title.

INDEX

Answer Key: **1.** Answers will vary; **2.** Answers will vary; **3.** B; **4.** C

28 DAY LOAN

**Hewlett-Woodmere Public Library
Hewlett, New York 11557**

**Business Phone 516-374-1967
Recorded Announcements 516-374-1667
Website www.hwpl.org**